Welcome to a world of fascinating stories and literary discoveries!

At EliMi, we strive to make your literary experience even more special and meaningful.

We would love to hear your opinion about our books. This will allow us to understand your tastes and needs, and will help us select the books that will interest you most in the future.

We invite you to leave a review of our books on the platform.
What were the aspects that you liked the most?
Is there anything we can improve on?

Your feedback is invaluable to us and will help us continue to deliver content that excites and inspires you.

Thank you for being part of this exciting literary adventure with us!

INDEX

Main Characters:

Javier Robles: A 36-year-old man with an impeccable appearance. In everyone's eyes, he is the ideal husband: successful, loving and responsible. However, beneath that facade of an exemplary husband, he leads a secret and dark life that makes him someone completely different outside the home.

Clara García: Javier's wife. A 34-year-old woman, tender, loyal and deeply in love with her husband. She is completely unaware of the double life he leads, blindly trusting the man she thinks she knows.

Lucía: A mysterious 27-year-old girl whom Javier meets in his secret life. She is cunning, manipulative and plays a key role in the part of Javier's life that he keeps hidden.

Natalia: A private detective, hired by Clara when she begins to suspect that something is not right. As the story progresses, her investigation will lead her to discover shocking truths.

Chapter 1: The Familiar Face

Javier Robles had always been an exemplary man. In the eyes of anyone who knew him superficially, he was the perfect model of a devoted husband, a successful professional and a respectable citizen.

His life seemed precisely calculated: from his impeccable appearance to his kind smile, every aspect of Javier was carefully assembled like the pieces of a puzzle that left no doubt about his character.

Clara, his wife, admired him. She loved to tell her friends how lucky she was to have found a man like him: loving, responsible and attentive.

Every morning, Javier left the house with a kiss on the forehead from Clara, a gesture that had become part of his almost mechanical routine. His briefcase in his hand, his shirt perfectly ironed, and a calm smile that hid much more than any casual observer could imagine.

However, the truth behind Javier Robles was darker than anyone suspected.

As he walked away from the warm atmosphere of his home and drove through the city streets, Javier was transformed.

His thoughts, until then focused on keeping up appearances, began to get lost in the life he led in parallel, a life in which he was neither the perfect husband nor the predictable man that everyone knew.

A notification on his cell phone vibrated silently in his pocket as he approached the city center.

The message was short and direct: "See you at 7."

And with those simple words, Javier's perfect routine vanished to give way to a completely different side of his being.

That secret life, one in which rules didn't matter and family responsibilities didn't exist, drew him in with an irresistible force.

Chapter 2: Shadows in the City

Javier drove silently through streets that seemed alien to his everyday world. The buildings, lights and hustle and bustle of the nighttime city seemed to be part of a stage designed exclusively for his other life.

The emotions that surfaced in this space were different: here there was no domestic love or promises of eternal loyalty. Here, Javier Robles was not the loving husband or the man of principles. He was someone completely different, someone that even he, in moments of lucidity, was afraid to acknowledge.

He parked his car on a side street, making sure to be away from any prying eyes.

Every time he went out to meet Lucía, the young woman who represented everything forbidden and liberating in his life, he did so with a mixture of excitement and guilt. He was aware of the risks, of the danger that Clara would discover what really happened during those long nights away from home. But despite his fear, Javier couldn't help himself.

Lucia was waiting for him at the corner of the bar where they usually met.

Tall, slim and with a magnetic presence, she was the kind of woman who seemed capable of enveloping anyone in her mystery.

For her, Javier was not a married man, he was not someone bound by promises or by duty. He was just a man who was looking for something more, something he couldn't find in his daily life. And she knew how to take advantage of it.

As he sat down in front of her, Javier dropped the mask of responsibility.

Here, in the gloom of the city, he could be the man he never allowed himself to be at home.

The conversations with Lucía were not about family or work; they were intense, almost dangerous, as if they were both playing with fire and enjoying the heat they gave off.

Lucia didn't ask questions about her personal life. I accepted him as he was at that moment, without ties, without expectations.

But Javier knew he couldn't go on like this forever. He knew that sooner or later the shadows he had created around him would begin to crumble, threatening to destroy everything he had once built.

Chapter 3: Clara and the Doubts

Clara García had been married to Javier for more than ten years, and had always considered her marriage a blessing.

From the beginning, Javier had been everything she had hoped for in a husband: loving, reliable, someone she could lean on.

However, over the past few months, something had changed. Clara couldn't pinpoint exactly when she had started noticing the little details that didn't fit, but she knew something was wrong.

The first clue came one night when Javier returned home late without a clear explanation.

Clara didn't think anything of it at the time. Javier was a busy man; his job often took him to last-minute meetings.

But over time, those nights of absence began to become more frequent. And it wasn't just the fact that he came home late. It was the way he did it, with a distant, almost evasive attitude.

When she asked him how his day had been, he answered in monosyllables, as if he were avoiding deeper conversation.

One afternoon, while organizing some papers in Javier's office, Clara found something she didn't expect: a receipt from an expensive restaurant, a place they had never been to together.

The date on the receipt coincided with one of those nights when Javier had returned late, claiming he had been in a work meeting. Her heart began to pound. She knew she shouldn't jump to conclusions, but doubt had already begun to creep into her mind.

That night, Clara observed Javier more closely.

He, as usual, acted as if nothing had changed. He asked her about her day, smiled at her as always, but something in his gaze was different. It was a subtle distance, something Clara hadn't seen before. What was going on? Was it possible that the man she had loved and trusted for so many years was hiding something from her?

As the weeks passed, doubt became a constant companion. Clara couldn't help but feel that Javier was not the same.

And although her heart wanted to deny it, her mind was beginning to consider a possibility that terrified her: what if Javier had a secret life that she knew nothing about?

Chapter 4: The Mask That Weighs

Javier found himself trapped in a duality of his own making. During the day, he was the perfect husband, the man everyone admired for his dedication to his family and his work. But at night, when the world around him shut down, he transformed into someone completely different.

That other life, the one he lived outside of Clara's and society's expectations, had become an addiction. The adrenaline he felt when moving between both worlds kept him going, but it also slowly consumed him.

The weight of the lies was beginning to become unbearable.

Every time he came home after a night with Lucia, he felt as if a part of him was falling apart.

Clara's smile when she welcomed him home, the warmth of her hug, all of that reminded him of the person he should be, but who was becoming increasingly difficult for him to be.

Inside him, guilt and adrenaline collided, creating an emotional chaos from which he could not escape. That night, Clara was waiting for him in the living room, reading a book as the clock struck ten.

When Javier walked in, he immediately noticed something wasn't right. The way she looked at him, her eyes searching him as if trying to find something hidden in his expression, put him on alert. "How was your day?" she asked, trying to keep the conversation light, but Javier sensed the weight of suspicion in her voice.

"Fine, just a little tired," he replied, trying hard to sound natural.

But Clara wasn't convinced. As the days passed, her suspicions grew, and although she wanted to trust him, something in her instinct told her that there was more to it than Javier was showing her.

Javier knew he was walking on thin ice, but he couldn't stop yet. He had gone too far.

Chapter 5: The Fracture of Silence

The air in Javier's house was becoming increasingly dense and heavy.

Clara, though always attentive, was beginning to withdraw, observing more than participating. Javier, for his part, kept up the facade, but inside he felt that the wall between him and his wife was growing higher every day.

The sound of the alarm clock brought him out of his thoughts. Clara no longer woke him with the gentle touch of her hand as before, she simply got up and began her day in silence.

During breakfast, the two limited themselves to exchanging short words, monosyllables that filled the void of a conversation that did not want to take place.

While driving to work, Javier's mind wandered between the two lives he led.

With Lucía, things were different. There were no questions, no inquisitive glances, just moments stolen from time. But even with Lucía, Javier was beginning to feel the pressure. How long could he keep everything hidden? He was one step away from everything collapsing, and that thought kept him on constant alert.

At work, things were no better. He had become more reserved, less willing to socialize with his colleagues. His performance had begun to decline, something his superiors had already noticed.

Javier knew he needed to focus more, but the feeling of being constantly watched was consuming him. Not only was he afraid that Clara would discover his double life, but the same darkness that enveloped him at home was beginning to seep into every aspect of his existence.

Chapter 6: Lucia's Shadows

That afternoon, Javier had a date with Lucía. At first, their encounters were sporadic, almost accidental. But as time went by, those moments had become a necessity.

Lucía was an escape, a refuge that allowed him to disconnect from the responsibility and weight of his marriage. However, even in that parallel life, Javier began to notice changes.

Lucia, who had been a carefree companion at first, was beginning to be more demanding, more demanding. She wanted to know more about Javier's life, about his thoughts, his fears. Although she said she didn't want to get too involved, her questions suggested otherwise. And although Javier was worried about the possibility that Lucia was looking for something more than furtive moments, he couldn't deny that he was still attracted to her.

They met at a café in a remote part of the city, as they usually did. Lucia arrived late, which was unusual for her, and her expression was more serious than usual.

"Javier, we need to talk," he said bluntly as he sat down.

Javier felt a knot form in his stomach. That phrase, coming from Lucia's lips, sounded dangerous. He tried hard to remain calm.

"What is it about?" he asked, trying to sound nonchalant.

Lucia looked into his eyes, searching for something in his expression, some sign that they shared the same concern.

—We can't go on like this. I want to know more about you, about what's really going on in your life. I don't want to be just a part of your shadows anymore —her words fell like a hammer on Javier.

For a second, the air seemed to disappear from the place. Javier knew that if Lucía started to demand more, things would get complicated. If until that moment he had managed to keep his double life intact, it was because both worlds remained separate. But if Lucía crossed that line, the structure he had built would begin to crack.

"There's nothing more to know, Lucia," he replied, with a smile that tried to hide his concern. "What we have is enough, isn't it?"

She didn't answer immediately. She looked at Javier with a mixture of distrust and disappointment.

"What if it isn't?" he finally asked, leaving the question hanging.

Javier felt the control he had fought so hard to maintain begin to slip through his fingers.

Chapter 7: Clara and the Hiring

While Javier was immersed in the chaos of his relationship with Lucía, Clara continued with her secret investigation.

After weeks of doubting and fighting her own fears, she had finally decided to take action. She couldn't continue living with uncertainty. She needed answers, and she knew there was only one way to get them.

Hiring a private detective hadn't been an easy decision. Clara had spent entire nights without sleep, debating with herself whether it was the right thing to do. What if she was wrong? What if Javier was simply stressed out by work, and she was seeing things that weren't there?

But the restaurant receipt remained etched in his mind. That piece of evidence, however small, had planted a doubt he couldn't ignore.

And so, one afternoon, she found herself sitting across from a calm, professional-looking woman named Natalia.

Natalia was a private detective with years of experience. Her reputation preceded her: discreet, efficient, and with an impeccable track record in solving delicate cases like Clara's.

"What I'm looking for is simple," Clara said, nervously playing with her hands. "I just want to know the truth."

Natalia watched her carefully, measuring her words before answering.—

The truth is not always what we expect to hear, he warned her. But if you are determined, I will begin immediately.

Clara nodded, although inside she felt a knot in her stomach. She knew that once Natalia started investigating, there would be no turning back.

Chapter 8: The Hunt Begins

Natalia was a meticulous professional.

From the moment Clara left her office, she got to work. The first thing she did was to routinely track Javier's movements. She began by observing his work schedules, his departures and arrivals home, and any behavior that might seem unusual.

The first few weeks were quiet, almost boring. Javier seemed like an ordinary man, with nothing to hide. But Natalia knew that appearances could be deceiving. Men like Javier knew how to cover their tracks, how to move in the shadows without leaving a trace. So, instead of rushing, she armed herself with patience.

Finally, her efforts paid off. One afternoon, watching from her car parked on a nearby street, she saw Javier leaving his office earlier than usual. She discreetly followed him to a more remote neighborhood, where she saw him enter a small café. Natalia parked at a safe distance and watched.

It wasn't long before a young woman, who was not Clara, came and sat next to him.

Natalia took photos from a distance, capturing every moment. She knew this woman was key, that she represented the life Javier was hiding from his wife.

The tension in the air was palpable. Javier and the woman, whom Natalia would later identify as Lucia, were talking in low voices, their expressions serious. They weren't just furtive lovers. There was something else, something deeper and more dangerous at play.

Natalia knew that with these tests, Clara would have what she was looking for. But she also knew that what Clara would receive could destroy her.

Chapter 9: The First Strike

When Natalia finally contacted Clara to show her the photos, Clara felt the ground beneath her feet crumble. Seeing Javier sitting in that café, laughing and talking to another woman, was like a stab in the back of her neck. The woman he was giving those smiles to, those glances, was not her.

And in that instant, Clara knew that her worst fears had come true.

The decision to confront Javier was not immediate. Clara needed time to assimilate what she had just discovered. But she also knew that she could not remain silent for long. The truth had come to light, and now it remained to be seen whether her marriage would survive it.

Chapter 10: The Search for Truth

Clara sat in her kitchen, a cup of cold coffee in her hands, as memories of happy times with Javier mixed with the bitter reality she had just discovered.

The images of him and Lucia in the café never left his mind. The laughter, the complicity, everything he had once considered exclusive to his marriage.

Every sip of coffee reminded her of what she had lost. Clara began to question every detail, every conversation, every glance. How many times had she ignored the signs?

The silence at home had become a refuge from her fear, and now that same house felt like a prison. She needed answers, not just for herself, but also to know what she was willing to do.

Finally, she decided she couldn't wait any longer. She had accumulated enough information to confront Javier.

It wouldn't be an easy conversation; she knew the pain would be overwhelming, but her need for clarity outweighed her fear.

Chapter 11: The Confrontation

That night, Javier arrived late, as he had done so many times in the past few weeks. Clara was waiting for him in the living room, the soft light from the sofa illuminating her figure. When Javier entered, he immediately felt the tension in the air. The room was silent, a silence heavy with unspoken words.

—Clara, I'm... —he began, but she interrupted him.

—Sit down, Javier. We need to talk.

Clara's voice was firm, but Javier sensed the trembling she was trying to hide. That moment had come, and he knew he couldn't escape the inevitable. He sat down on the opposite chair, feeling the weight of his own lie begin to crush him.

"I've been watching, Javier," Clara said, her voice barely a whisper, but with an echo of determination.

—. I saw the photos. With her.

Javier fell silent, unable to find the right words. His heart was pounding; he knew the truth had been revealed and his world was about to fall apart.

"What... what do you want me to say?" he finally stammered, the mask of confidence beginning to fade.

Clara leaned forward, her eyes locked with his. Disappointment and sadness were reflected in her gaze.

—I want the truth, Javier. I want to know what's going on. Why did you lie to me?

The question pierced her like a spear. Javier felt his throat close up. Every word he had planned in his mind was fading away. The reality of his situation was confronting him in a way he had never imagined.

"I didn't want this to happen. I didn't want to hurt you," he replied, guilt tightening his chest. "It was a mistake, Clara. I didn't want it to turn out like this."

Clara looked at him in disbelief. It was as if his words only deepened the wound.

"A mistake? A mistake?!" he cried, his voice rising. "Is that how you see it? I've given everything for you, for us, and you've chosen another life."

The silence that followed was deafening. Anger and sadness intertwined in the air.

Javier knew he should try to explain, but the words seemed to get stuck in his throat.

"I don't know what else to say. I'm just... sorry," he murmured at last, but Clara didn't want to listen anymore.

Chapter 12: The Storm

Clara felt tears well up in her. But she didn't want to cry in front of him; she didn't want him to see her weakness.

He stood up abruptly and began to pace the room, searching his mind for a way to understand what he had just discovered. The rage in his chest burned like an uncontrolled fire.

"How could you do that?" he asked, his voice shaking between fury and pain. "What are you missing in this life? Aren't you happy with me?"

Clara's words made Javier feel a punch in the stomach. The truth was that he had lost his way. In his search for an emotion he had stopped feeling, he had destroyed what he valued most.

"I didn't know how to say it," he said finally, his voice full of desperation. "I thought I could handle it. I thought I could have it all."

The disbelief in Clara's eyes turned to disdain.

"Everything? What is 'everything'? A life with two women?" he said, his tone heavy with irony. "You have chosen this path, Javier, and now you have to face the consequences."

At that moment, Javier understood that he had crossed a threshold from which he could not return. His life, the one he had built with Clara, was about to fall apart, and he was the architect of his own ruin.

Chapter 13: The Decision

After that confrontation, Clara felt caught in a whirlwind of emotions. She needed to get out of the house, away from Javier, from her pain, from his empty promises.

That night, she decided the only way to find clarity was to give the situation a break. She went for a walk through the deserted streets of the city. The flickering lights and distant murmur of the nightlife surrounded her, but she felt completely alone. In her mind, her life with Javier played out like a movie, each scene more painful than the last.

As he walked, his thoughts returned to Lucia. Who was she really? What did she mean to Javier? This woman who had managed to draw out of him a part that she believed was exclusive to her marriage. He wondered if Lucia had also been a victim of Javier's lies or if she was simply an accomplice willing to play a dangerous game.

Clara decided she couldn't stay in the darkness of her confusion. She needed answers. And to find them, she had to face Lucia.

Chapter 14: Meeting in the Dark

Clara searched the Internet until she found the café where Javier had been seen with Lucia. She knew he could be there that night. With each step towards the place, adrenaline coursed through her body. She had decided that she couldn't be the victim in this story; she had to claim her power.

The café was a cozy place, filled with warm lights and murmurs. Clara sat in a corner, hiding her nervousness as she watched the door. She didn't know what to expect, but her determination kept her going.

When she finally saw Lucia enter, she felt her heart race. The woman entered with unwavering confidence, oblivious to the gathering storm. Clara wondered if Lucia knew of her existence, if she was aware of the chaos she had unleashed in her life.

Lucia walked to the bar, and Clara decided it was time to act. She stood up and walked over to her, feeling the tension rising with each step.

"Lucia?" he said, causing the young woman to turn around in surprise.

Lucia's gaze darkened instantly. She was aware of what this meant, and her smile disappeared.

"Clara?" he asked, his voice low and tense.

Clara couldn't let fear get the better of her. She had come for answers, and she wasn't going to stop now.

—I need to talk to you. You and me, now.

The determination in Clara's voice was palpable. Lucia nodded slowly, and they both headed towards a table away, where the conversation that would change the course of their lives was about to begin.

Chapter 15: The Naked Truth

Clara and Lucia sat in a corner of the café, the tension between them palpable.

Clara took a deep breath, searching for the courage she needed to face the woman who had embodied her deepest fears.

"Thank you for agreeing to talk to me," Clara began, though her voice was a whisper laden with emotion. "I'm not here to fight, but we need to understand each other."

Lucia stared at her, a mix of surprise and caution in her gaze. The confusion on her face was evident.

—I... don't know what to say. This isn't easy —Lucia replied, trying to find the right words.

"It's not for me either," Clara replied, letting the pain that consumed her show. "I know you're with Javier. I saw it, and I can no longer ignore what that means. But before you continue, I need you to tell me the truth."

Clara's words collided in the air, and Lucia fell silent, as if each word carried an unbearable weight. Finally, she gathered her courage.

"I'm sorry," she said, her voice shaking. "I didn't know you were his wife when we started dating. Javier... he never told me about you. He told me he was lonely, that he'd left his life behind."

Clara felt the ground move beneath her feet. Lucia's words, though surprising, were also a reflection of the manipulation Javier had carried out.

"Do you really think he told you the truth?" Clara asked, unable to hide the disbelief in her voice. "Javier is a master at deception."

Lucia nodded, her face paling.

—I didn't want to believe it. I wanted to think that what we had was real. But now... I understand that I've been a part of something I shouldn't have touched.

Clara felt a pang of compassion, but also of rage. Lucia was not the only victim in this story, but she was also part of the pain she was feeling.

"And what do you plan to do now?" Clara asked, her voice firmer now. "Are you going to keep seeing him?"

"I don't know," Lucia replied, her gaze lost on the ground. "I don't want to hurt anyone, but I can't keep living this lie. I don't know if I can trust him after what you said."

The two women shared a silence that seemed endless. The tension in the air was mixed with sadness and betrayal. Clara understood that Lucía had also been deceived, but the anger she felt towards Javier continued to burn.

"If you leave him, if you decide to break up with him, make sure he knows why you're doing it," Clara said, her tone firm. "I don't want him to continue his double life, to continue hurting more people."

Lucia looked up, her eyes shining with tears that threatened to spill over.

—I will. I can't be a part of this anymore. But what about you? What will you do, Clara?

Lucia's questions collided in Clara's mind. It was a difficult question, one that still had no answer. Should she try to save her marriage or let it fall apart as it deserved?

"I don't know," Clara admitted, feeling sadness enveloping her. "But I have to think about myself. This can't go on."

Chapter 16: The Meeting with Javier

After her conversation with Lucia, Clara returned home with mixed feelings. She knew that her life was about to change drastically, but she couldn't foresee how it would all unfold.

 When she entered the house, Javier was waiting for her in the living room, a nervous expression on his face.

—Clara, I have to talk to you —he began, but she interrupted him.

—No, Javier. This is not the time for your explanations. I've been talking to Lucía.

Her voice sounded like a shot, and the pallor on Javier's face was evident. He tried to process the information, but Clara didn't give him time.

—She told me what's going on between you two. I can't believe you were so selfish. How could you deceive me like that?

Javier stood up, his face reflecting a mixture of shock and guilt.

—Clara, let me explain. It wasn't like that... —her voice trembled, but Clara wasn't willing to listen to any more lies.

"I don't need any more excuses!" she shouted, feeling anger welling up from deep within her. "You've ruined everything, Javier. This marriage has become a lie, and I'm tired of living in the dark."

Javier moved towards her, but Clara stepped back, her body filled with defensiveness.

—No, don't come closer. I don't want to hear your empty words. I can't believe anything you say.

At that moment, Javier realized there was no way to repair the damage. He had crossed a line, and his world, which he had built with such care, was falling apart.

—Clara, please... —her voice was a whisper, almost broken.

—I don't want anything else from you. I need time to think, to decide what I want to do with my life —Clara replied, and with those words, she felt that she was finally taking control of her destiny.

Without waiting for an answer, Clara left the room, leaving Javier standing in the darkness of his own deception.

The confrontation had left deep marks on both of them, and although the future was uncertain, Clara knew she could not allow the pain to define her.

Chapter 17: Refuge in Solitude

That night, Clara retreated into her room, surrounded by the silence that had once been her home. The walls that had once made her feel safe now seemed to scream her pain. She felt overwhelmed by confusion and fear, but there was also a spark of release.

As she sat on the bed, hands on her knees, she began to reflect on her life. She had let Javier dominate her thoughts, her feelings, her everything. It was time to take back her voice, to make decisions that would benefit her.

Over time, her mind began to calm down, and she realized she needed an outlet, a way to rebuild her life away from Javier's shadows. She thought about her forgotten dreams, about the things she had put aside in order to be the perfect wife.

She decided it was time to rewrite her story. She would begin to do what she had always wanted to do: explore her passions, rediscover who she was, and leave the weight of betrayal behind.

Clara closed her eyes, imagining a future where the light shone again, where she was once again the master of her destiny.

Chapter 18: The Echo of Guilt

Javier stood in the living room, feeling the emptiness take over him. Clara's words still echoed in his mind, a constant echo of her betrayal. As the night progressed, despair became a constant companion. He knew he had crossed a line, and the possibility of losing Clara became more real with each passing second.

He sat on the couch, the darkness of the place enveloping him. The house that had been his refuge now felt like a prison. He remembered the happy times they had shared, the laughter in the kitchen, the movie nights. It had all vanished in an instant, replaced by pain and betrayal.

Javier reached for his phone, contemplating the idea of sending a message to Lucia. But he instantly stopped himself. He couldn't continue like this, dragging more people into his chaos. He knew he had to face the consequences of his actions.

Chapter 19: The Unexpected Call

The next morning, Javier woke up with a cloudy mind. Clara had left the house, and he felt more alone than ever.

He decided he needed to talk to someone, someone who could help him understand how he had gotten to this point. Without thinking, he dialed Lucia's number.

The doorbell rang several times before she answered. Lucia's voice sounded tired, almost fearful.

"Javier?" she asked, her tone indicating that she wasn't sure she wanted to talk to him.

"I need to talk to you," Javier said, his voice full of urgency. "I don't know what to do. Clara is really hurt, and I... I've been an idiot."

Lucia took a deep breath, and Javier could hear the internal struggle in her voice.

—I don't know if we should talk. This is complicated, Javier.

—I know, but I need to understand. Why did I let this happen? Everything has gone so far, and now I realize that I have ruined my life.

Lucia was silent for a moment. Finally, she said:

—I don't think there's an easy answer. But I'll tell you: your actions have consequences. Not just for you, but for Clara, for me.

Lucia's words were a direct blow. Javier realized that each decision had woven a web of pain that trapped him.

—I'm going to try to talk to Clara. I can't let this end like this.

Lucia sighed, a sound full of resignation.

—That's right. But don't expect me to forgive you easily. Neither will she.

Javier felt overwhelmed, knowing that the battle had only just begun. But he was determined to do whatever it took to right his wrongs.

Chapter 20: The Search for Redemption

That same afternoon, Javier went to the park where they used to walk together. He felt nervous and full of doubts. The image of Clara, hurt and disappointed, haunted him. He knew that facing her would be the hardest thing he had ever done, but also the most necessary.

When he arrived, the cool air hit his face. He sat on a bench, watching the couples pass by. In their eyes, he saw what he had lost.

Finally, after what seemed like an eternity, Clara appeared. Her figure was silhouetted against the setting sun, and Javier felt a pang in his heart.

"Clara," he said, standing up, "I need to talk to you."

She looked at him suspiciously, but approached slowly.

—I don't want to argue any further, Javier. I've already said what I needed to say.

"I know," he replied, his voice full of sincerity. "But I need to explain. I need you to understand why I did what I did."

Clara frowned, and for a moment, silence became a chasm between them.

—And what are you going to tell me? That I wasn't what I seemed? That you didn't love me? —Her tone was biting, but there was a hint of sadness in her eyes.

"No, Clara. I love you. That's what hurts the most. I got lost in a world of lies and now I'm here, trying to face what I've done," he said, feeling vulnerability wash over him. "I never wanted to hurt you."

Clara stared at him, and Javier could see the tears in her eyes.

—But you did it, Javier. And that can't be erased with words.

The truth was overwhelming, but Javier knew he had to move on.

—I know I can't change what I've done, but I want to try to make amends. I'm willing to do whatever it takes. I want to seek help, talk to a therapist...

Clara interrupted him.

—And that's going to solve everything? Are you going to promise me you won't do it again?

—I can't promise you that, Clara. But I can promise you that I'm willing to fight for us. I want to learn to be the man you deserve.

The air was charged with tension as Clara looked at him, evaluating his words. The internal battle in her heart was palpable. Javier felt time stop.

"I don't know if I'm ready to forgive, but I appreciate that you're here and that you want to fight," Clara finally said, her voice softer. "But this won't be easy."

Javier nodded, feeling the small light of hope beginning to light up. It was a long road, but he was determined to take it, not only for Clara, but for himself.

Chapter 21: Clara's Decision

That night, Clara returned home with her mind in turmoil. Although she had taken a small step toward reconciliation, there was still a great distance between them. She needed time to process everything that had happened, but she knew she couldn't live in the shadow of her pain.

She sat at her desk, surrounded by papers and memories. She decided that she should write down her thoughts. As she did so, she began to clear her mind.

"I am hurt. But I don't want this hurt to define me. I must find my way, even if I am alone."

The words flowed from her pen, and as she wrote, she realized that the decision to move forward was hers. She couldn't allow herself to get lost in the pain of betrayal. She needed to find her voice, her strength.

As she wrote, a feeling of determination began to grow within her.

Clara knew there was still a long way to go. The possibility of forgiving Javier existed, but she also knew that she had to prioritize her well-being.

She decided it was time to seek support, to talk to someone who could help her understand her feelings. Doing this didn't mean she was turning her back on Javier, but rather putting herself first.

Chapter 22: The Accident

Clara left the house one rainy morning, seeking clarity in the fog that had covered her life. After the conversation with Javier, although she had decided to give him a chance to redeem himself, she knew that she still needed space to think.

Riding in her car, raindrops hit the windshield, creating a rhythm that reflected the chaos in her mind.

She drove aimlessly through the city, lost in her thoughts. The rain was getting heavier, and the roads were getting slippery. As she tried to change lanes, a car sped up behind her. Clara tried to brake, but the wet pavement caused her to lose control.

It all happened in a matter of seconds: the sound of metal against metal, the air exploding in a single sharp bang, and the world spinning around him.
Her head hit the steering wheel, and darkness took over.

Chapter 23: The Discovery

When Clara woke up, everything was a blur. The white light of the hospital blinded her eyes, and the beeping of the machines around her slowly brought her back to reality. Her body was in pain, but what disturbed her most was the feeling of emptiness in her chest. She didn't remember how she got there. Only fragments of the accident jumbled together in her mind.

A nurse appeared in his field of vision, smiling softly.

"How are you feeling?" he asked in a calm voice. "You've been here for a few hours, but you're stable. It was a bad accident, but you were lucky."

Clara nodded, still a little disoriented, when the door opened and the doctor entered with a file in his hand. He approached the bed and, after checking her vital signs, paused for a moment before speaking.

"Clara, there's something we need to discuss," he said in a serious but comforting voice. "When you arrived at the hospital, we decided to run some tests to make sure there were no internal injuries. During one of those tests, we discovered something unexpected: you're pregnant."

Clara's world seemed to stop. The doctor's words echoed in her head, over and over again.

Pregnant. She hadn't planned this, hadn't even thought about the possibility after everything she'd been through with Javier. She felt like she couldn't breathe for a moment.

"How long?" she asked in a whisper.

"You're about eight weeks along," the doctor replied. "The most important thing now is that the baby is doing well, despite the accident. We've done some tests and there are no signs of complications."

Clara fell silent, processing the news.

His body had reacted, but his mind still couldn't process it.

A son. Amidst the chaos, a new beginning was growing inside her, but along with the joy of the life she was leading, a heart-wrenching fear invaded her. She couldn't let Javier know. Not now.

Chapter 24: A Difficult Decision

The days in the hospital were long and silent. Clara didn't let anyone else know about her pregnancy. When Javier came to see her, worried after learning of the accident, she remained calm, deliberately hiding the truth.

"I'm fine, it was just a scare," she told him as he approached the bed, taking her hand. "The doctors told me it wasn't serious. I just need to rest."

Javier looked at her with a mix of guilt and relief. Even though their relationship was still broken, his concern was genuine, and that only made Clara's decision more complicated.

"I'm glad you're okay. You don't know how scared I was," Javier said, trying to sound stronger than he really felt. "I want to help you with whatever you need."

Clara forced a smile. She knew that, at that moment, Javier couldn't be a part of this secret. There was too much uncertainty between them. She didn't want him to use the pregnancy as an excuse to hold on to a broken relationship.

—I just need time, Javier. Right now, it's best that we both have some space —she replied, looking out the window, avoiding his eyes.

Javier, though confused, accepted her wish to distance himself. He didn't want to pressure her, not after everything he'd done. So he left the hospital that night, with more questions than answers, while Clara remained in her bed, clinging to her secret.

Chapter 25: The Double Burden of Silence

Weeks passed, and Clara was discharged.

She returned home, but not to the life she had left behind. She was determined to keep her pregnancy a secret for the time being. The doubt remained in her heart: should she tell Javier? Every time she saw him, she felt the weight of her double life.

The pregnancy progressed, and as her body began to change, so did her outlook.

Sometimes, on nights when she was alone, she found herself caressing her belly, feeling a deep connection with the little being growing inside her.

Chapter 26: The Encounter with the True Clara

In the midst of her loneliness, Clara decided to seek professional help. She began attending therapy sessions to process the whirlwind of emotions that engulfed her.

In one such session, her therapist, a soft-spoken older woman, asked her point-blank:
—Clara, what do you really want? Not what you think you should do, or what others expect. What do you need? The question resonated with Clara.

For months she had been moving between pain, guilt and doubt, without stopping to really think about what she wanted. In that moment, as tears ran down her face, she realized something important: she wanted to be happy, free, and protect her son from the chaos she had been immersed in.

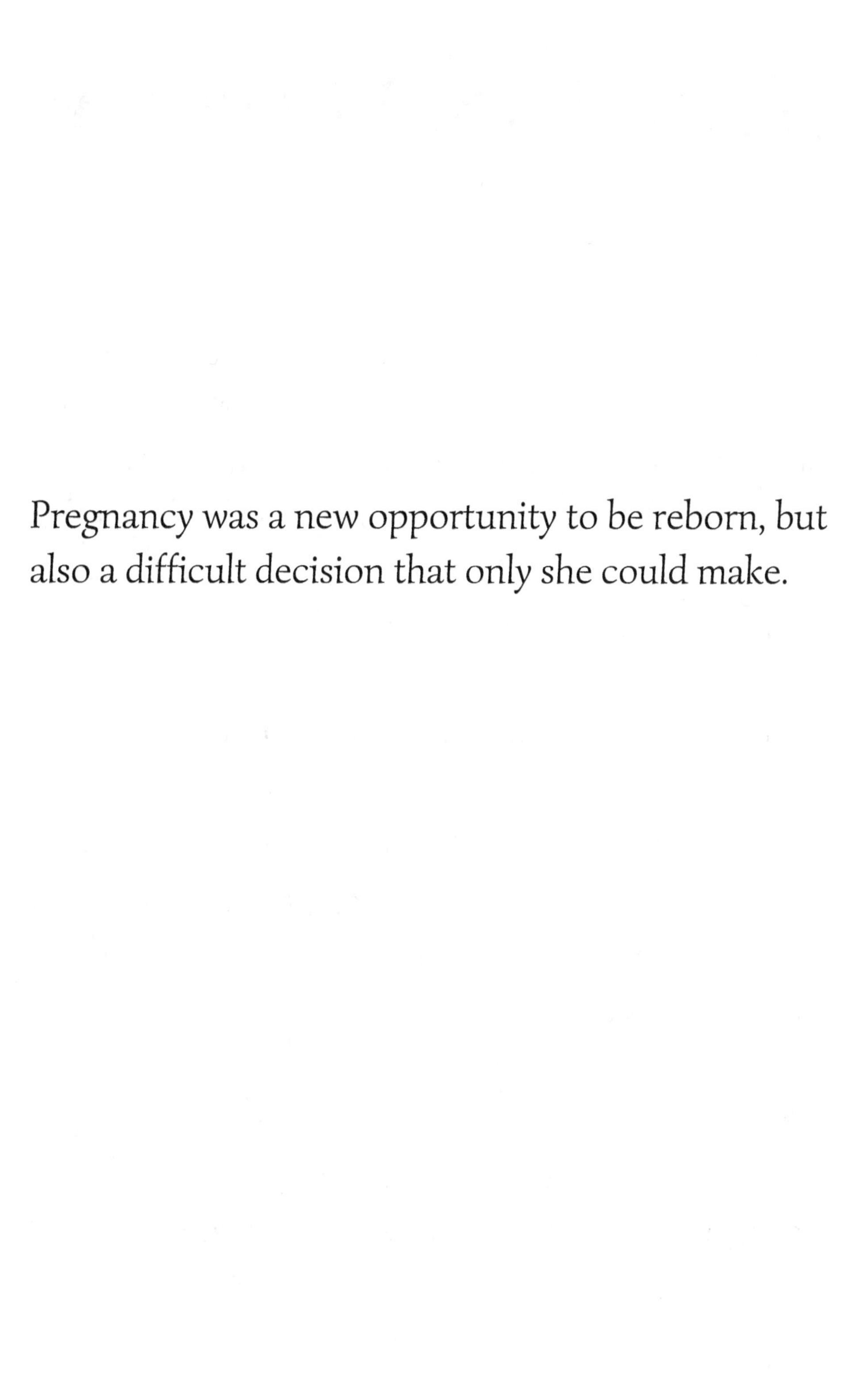

Pregnancy was a new opportunity to be reborn, but also a difficult decision that only she could make.

Chapter 27: Clara Takes the Reins

After weeks of reflection, Clara made a decision: she wouldn't tell Javier anything for the moment. She needed to protect herself and the baby. She knew Javier was trying to make amends for his mistakes, but she still didn't trust him enough to share such a deep secret.

Clara began planning her future, looking at how she could become a mother and rebuild her life. She surrounded herself with supportive friends, but always kept her pregnancy private. She didn't want anyone else to interfere with her decision until she was completely sure.

With each passing day, she felt a stronger connection to the baby, and with that connection, her strength grew. She knew she could do it alone if she needed to.

It was a reminder that despite all the chaos, something beautiful could still blossom.

But there was also fear.

What would it be like to be a mother in the midst of a crumbling marriage? How could she raise a child with someone she didn't know she could trust? The idea that Javier might use the baby as a way to keep her tied down terrified her.

Chapter 28: Javier's Restlessness

Javier felt that something was out of place. Since the accident, Clara seemed more distant, more reserved. Although he had tried to get closer, something in her behavior had changed, and he couldn't shake the feeling that she was hiding something from him.

It wasn't just the cold between them anymore, something deeper was brewing beneath the surface.

He watched Clara avoid certain topics and her gaze drift away from conversations that would once have been normal. Sometimes he saw her unconsciously touch her belly, as if protecting something, and a pang of doubt began to form in his mind. Was it just paranoia or was there really something Clara wasn't telling him?

Javier, still trying to redeem himself for his betrayal, decided not to confront her right away. He wanted to give her space, but the uncertainty was eating away at him.

He spent his nights reviewing the signs in his mind, trying to understand what Clara was hiding. The distance between them couldn't just be the result of the accident or the previous conflict. There was something else, something important.

Chapter 29: The First Suspicions

One day, while Clara was out, Javier found himself alone at home, caught in a whirlwind of doubts.

He had decided to work from home to be more present, hoping to show Clara that he was committed to her and their relationship. But the more he tried to get closer, the more he felt she was pulling away.

That afternoon, while organizing some papers in the living room, a hospital envelope fell off the desk.

Opening it, he saw the medical report from Clara's accident. It was the same one he had already seen, but something new caught his eye: a section was marked confidential, a detail that had gone unnoticed in his previous reading. Javier frowned and felt a strange uneasiness in his chest.

He decided not to look any further, but his doubts continued to grow. What could be so important that Clara would hide it from him?

Chapter 30: Following the Clues

As the days passed, the distance between them became more evident. Javier tried to be patient, but he couldn't let go of the growing suspicion.

Clara began to cancel her outings with him, she spent more time away from home, and she often seemed more tired. Although he tried not to give it any importance, there were times when he saw a new fragility in her that he found strange.

One afternoon, while Clara was sleeping soundly after an outing, Javier noticed something that disconcerted him even more. On her nightstand, she had left a small notebook where she kept notes, something he had never seen before. Although he knew that reading it invaded her privacy, his protective instinct and growing distrust pushed him to open it.

The first few pages were notes about the accident and how he had felt in the days afterward, but it was when he got halfway through the notebook that something struck him like thunder: a passage in which Clara talked about her pregnancy. Javier felt his heart stop as he read the words.

Clara was pregnant, and she hadn't told him.

Chapter 31: Facing the Truth

The revelation left him in shock. As he reread Clara's words, pain and confusion mingled within him. Why had she kept it from him? What did that mean for their relationship?

Javier felt a mix of sadness and anger. Had it been so bad that she felt she couldn't trust him with something so important?

He spent the rest of the night in the living room, unable to sleep. His mind was filled with questions, all of them unanswered. The relationship was already on fragile ground, but this secret changed everything. He couldn't help but wonder if the pregnancy was the reason Clara was keeping him at a distance, if she was planning a life without him.

The next morning when Clara got up, she found Javier sitting at the table, his eyes tired and dark.

The silence between them was heavy. He knew he couldn't keep up the facade that everything was okay any longer.

"Clara," Javier began, his voice tense. "We need to talk."

She looked at him, knowing something important was about to come out of his mouth. In his eyes, she saw the storm of emotions that had been building up for days.

"About what?" he asked cautiously, his hand unconsciously touching her belly.

Javier sighed, feeling the weight of what he was about to say.
—Why didn't you tell me you were pregnant?

The question hung in the air, and Clara's face filled with surprise and fear. The moment she had so feared had arrived, and now she had no choice but to face it.

Chapter 32: The Confrontation

Clara felt the world stop for a moment. The secret she had kept so carefully was now out, and there was no turning back.

Javier's words were direct, but what disarmed her most was the expression in his eyes: a mix of sadness, disappointment and a desperate desire to understand.

"How do you know?" Clara asked, her voice shaking.

"I found out," Javier replied, avoiding telling her how. "But what I don't understand is why you didn't tell me. Were you planning to leave me out of this? What's going on, Clara?"

Clara looked down, unable to sustain the intensity of his gaze.

"It's not that simple, Javier," she said, feeling guilt creeping in. "Our relationship… is broken. I didn't know how to tell you. I didn't know if I wanted you to be in this. I wasn't ready to face everything."

—Weren't you ready to face it? Or were you not ready to tell me because you didn't trust me? —Javier stood up, pacing back and forth. —This baby is mine too! And if our relationship is broken, don't you think I at least deserved to know? We deserve to be able to decide together what to do!

Clara felt the weight of her decision fall on her shoulders. She knew Javier was partly right, but she was also terrified of trusting him again, of giving him something so valuable when the wound of his betrayal had not yet healed.

"I didn't want us to use this pregnancy as an excuse to fix what's broken between us," she finally confessed. "I didn't want you to feel like you had to stay alone because of the baby, because that's not going to solve our problems."

Javier stared at her, his breathing ragged. He was hurt, but he also understood Clara's fear.

—I don't want this to be an excuse, Clara. I want to be here, for you, for the baby. I don't know if we can fix this, but I want to be a part of this. I want to try, even if it's just for him... or for her.

Clara closed her eyes, feeling the tension slowly drain out of her. The fear of facing this truth had consumed her for weeks, but now that everything was on the table, she realized that although the path was uncertain, she was no longer alone in her decision.

Chapter 33: New Territories

With the truth finally revealed, Clara and Javier were left in new, uncertain territory. They knew that pregnancy would not solve the problems they had been carrying around from before, but they also recognized that this was a new beginning, although not entirely desired or planned.

The following weeks were a test of fire for both of them. They tried to coexist with the tension, looking for small moments of connection between the distance.

Clara still maintained her reservations, but something inside her was beginning to soften, acknowledging that maybe Javier really did want to change.

Chapter 34: The Consequences of Pregnancy

As Clara progressed through her pregnancy, the reality of her situation began to dawn on her. Morning sickness and fatigue were constant, but what overwhelmed her most were the conflicting emotions that assailed her daily.

 Javier was willing to be by her side, but she couldn't shake the feeling of betrayal that had marked their relationship.

While Clara struggled with her own heart, Javier tried to prove he was committed to being a good father. He offered to accompany her to doctor's appointments, helped with shopping, and was attentive to every detail.

However, every time Clara looked at him, she was reminded of his lies and his infidelity, and bitterness took hold of her.

Tensions began to mount. Clara felt caught between wanting a future for her son and being unable to forgive Javier.

Small arguments turned into big fights, and the atmosphere at home became heavy. Clara began to notice that, despite Javier's efforts, there was a wall that he couldn't break down.

Chapter 35: Separate Ways

Clara decided she needed a change of scenery.

The house where she had once dreamed of raising a family now felt like a prison.

So, after discussing it with her friends, she decided to temporarily move in with her mother. The idea of a space away from Javier brought her unexpected relief.

The move was emotional. Clara felt like she was leaving a part of her life behind, but she also knew it was necessary. As she organized her things at her mother's house, she experienced a new sense of freedom. Conversations with her mother and the unconditional support of her friends allowed her to explore her feelings without the weight of Javier's expectations.

However, Javier did not give up. Despite the physical distance, he continued to send her messages, asking about her well-being and trying to understand her decision. Clara, for her part, felt that she had made the right decision, but uncertainty and guilt plagued her.

The space between them became an abyss.

Javier began to face the reality of being a father, but without Clara's support.

He started attending support groups for expectant fathers, where other men shared their experiences. Although he found it uncomfortable at first, he soon realized that he was not alone in his struggle. Each story showed him that the path of fatherhood was full of uncertainties and that everyone had their own battles.

Chapter 36: The Echo of Decisions

While Javier looked for ways to adapt to his new reality, Clara focused on her health and well-being.

Visits to the doctor became a refuge, where she could focus on her baby's growth and the changes that were to come. However, there were times when the loneliness became overwhelming, and the emptiness of not having Javier by her side became palpable.

One day, while in the park with her mother, Clara saw a couple strolling with a stroller. The sight of the happy family struck her heart. What would have become of her if Javier had not betrayed her trust? The question tormented her, and every day she found herself more and more trapped in her own mind.

Clara decided to talk to her therapist about these feelings. During the session, she realized that forgiveness wasn't just a gift for Javier; it was a gift for herself. But the path to forgiveness seemed long and uncertain. Clara still felt like she wasn't ready to take that step.

Chapter 37: The Unexpected Visit

One day, while Clara was at her mother's house, she received an unexpected visitor. It was Javier. Her heart stopped for a moment; she hadn't expected to see him so soon. His expression was one of determination, but also of vulnerability. Clara felt overwhelmed, but she knew she couldn't keep running away.

"We need to talk," Javier said, his voice shaking slightly.

Clara nodded, feeling the air grow heavy around her. They sat down in the living room, and Javier began to talk about his feelings, about how difficult it had been to adjust to the new reality. But what worried him most was Clara and the baby's well-being.

"I've been attending a support group," he said, meeting her gaze. "I've learned a lot about parenting, but also about relationships. I want you to know that I'm here for you, for whatever you need."

Clara stared at him, recognizing the sincerity in his eyes. But her heart was still divided. Could she really trust him again?

—Javier, I don't know if I can do this. I don't know if I can forgive you. It still hurts —she replied, her voice breaking.

Javier felt like the world was falling apart around him. Time seemed to be against him, and Clara's words were a painful reminder of what he had lost.

But deep inside him, there was a spark of hope. He knew they had to face their demons, and he was ready to do so.

Chapter 38: A New Beginning

From that conversation, Clara and Javier began to build bridges. Although the path to reconciliation was uncertain, they both knew there was a baby on the way who deserved a chance.

They began to see each other more, attending medical appointments together and sharing moments, although there was still much to be resolved.

Yet despite her good intentions, Clara struggled with her own heart. Every time Javier smiled or made a kind gesture, an echo of the past reminded her of what she had lost.

Shared laughter was often overshadowed by memories of pain.

Javier, for his part, tried to be the man Clara needed, but every glance she gave him was a reminder that he had not yet earned her trust. The struggle between them became a delicate game of emotions and memories.

As the months passed, Clara realized that forgiveness didn't mean forgetting. It was a daily choice to let go of the pain and allow something new to blossom.

In the midst of the trials, they began to glimpse an uncertain future, but together.

Chapter 39: The Big Day

Finally, the day of birth arrived. Clara was admitted to the hospital, and while she waited, Javier was by her side, nervous and anxious. At that moment, all past differences and arguments seemed to fade away. Clara, surrounded by love and pain, felt stronger than ever.

The birth of the baby was a life-changing experience. Clara felt a mix of relief, love and fear. When she finally held her son in her arms, everything made sense. In that instant, she realized that even though their journey had been difficult, there was a new life that depended on them.

As she looked at her baby, Clara felt a spark of hope. Maybe all was not lost. Maybe, together, they could rebuild something new.

Chapter 40: New Horizons

After days in the hospital, Clara and Javier found themselves at home with their baby. It was the beginning of a new chapter, full of uncertainties, but also of new possibilities. The road to forgiveness would still be long, but they were both willing to walk it together.

Despite the scars of the past, they realized that every day was an opportunity to learn to love each other again, not only as a couple, but as parents.

Together, they would face the challenges that life presented to them, and although the road would not be easy, they knew that they would not have to travel it alone.

Chapter 41: New Routines

Days turned into weeks, and weeks into months. Life with their baby brought unexpected challenges. Clara and Javier faced sleep deprivation, worries, and endless nights of crying. But through it all, something beautiful began to blossom between them.

Each small moment shared became a brick in rebuilding their relationship. Javier took on his role as father with enthusiasm, and Clara viewed him with a mixture of admiration and love.

Little by little, memories of the past began to fade, replaced by laughter and complicity.

Chapter 41: New Routines

Days turned into weeks, and weeks into months. Life with their baby brought unexpected challenges. Clara and Javier faced sleep deprivation, worries, and endless nights of crying. But through it all, something beautiful began to blossom between them.

Each small moment shared became a brick in rebuilding their relationship. Javier took on his role as father with enthusiasm, and Clara viewed him with a mixture of admiration and love.

Little by little, memories of the past began to fade, replaced by laughter and complicity.

Chapter 42: Grandma's Visit

One day, Clara decided to invite her mother to meet her grandson. Excitement filled the air as they prepared the house. Javier was nervous, worried about how his mother-in-law would react. Clara, for her part, felt a mix of joy and anxiety. She knew her mother could be harsh, but she hoped she could see how their relationship had changed.

When his mother arrived, the hugs were warm, but the tension was palpable. Javier introduced himself with a genuine smile, but his mother's gaze was wary. However, upon seeing her grandson, all worry dissipated. The grandmother wrapped the baby in her arms, and the smiles began to flow.

During the visit, Clara and Javier realized that their love and commitment were not only visible between each other, but also in the way they cared for their son. It was a reminder that they could form a family despite their past.

Chapter 43: The Anniversary of the Accident

The anniversary of the accident was approaching, and Clara was feeling a mix of emotions.

It had been a year since her life changed drastically, and while there was pain in those memories, there was also growth. She decided she didn't want that day to just be a reminder of the bad. She wanted to celebrate it as a new beginning.

Clara suggested to Javier to have a small ceremony in the park where everything happened. She wanted to remember what they had overcome, and also what they had built. Javier accepted enthusiastically, and together they prepared a small picnic.

Chapter 44: The Ceremony

The day arrived, and the sun was shining softly. Clara and Javier carried the baby in his stroller, surrounded by an air of hope.

When they arrived at the park, they sat down in the same spot where Clara had had her accident. The view was beautiful, and the sound of birdsong filled the air.

Clara took a deep breath and began to speak. She explained how the accident had changed her, how she had learned to fight and find strength within herself.

There had been dark moments, but there had also been light. And in that light, she had found Javier.

—Today, I don't want to remember only the pain — Clara said, looking at Javier — I want to celebrate life, our son, and the journey we've taken together.

Javier looked at her with a mixture of love and admiration. In that instant, he knew that their relationship had not only survived, but had flourished.

Chapter 45: The Renewed Commitment

After sharing her thoughts, Clara pulled a small envelope from her purse. It was a symbolic certificate they had created together, a promise of renewed commitment. She handed it to Javier, who took it with trembling hands.

"We promise to work on this together, to be better for ourselves and for our son," Clara said, her eyes shining with excitement.

Javier, touched by the gesture, took Clara's hand and kissed it softly. At that moment, they both knew that, despite the obstacles, they were willing to build a future full of love and trust.

Chapter 46: The Final Revelation

As the ceremony progressed, Javier gathered his courage. There was something he wanted to share, something he had been holding back. He stood up, looking at Clara and the baby.

"I want to ask you for one more thing," he began, his voice firm. "This past year has been a roller coaster, but I am grateful for every moment, every struggle. Clara, I want to spend the rest of my life with you, building our family and creating memories together."

With that, he knelt down and pulled out a small engagement ring. Clara gaped, her eyes filled with tears of surprise and joy.
—Clara, will you marry me?

The world stopped for a moment.

Clara looked at Javier, remembering everything they had overcome, every tear and every laugh. And in that instant, she knew that their love was stronger than ever.

"Yes," she replied excitedly. "Yes, I do!"

Tears began to flow, and as Javier placed the ring on her finger, Clara felt the weight of the past fade away.

This was their new beginning.

Chapter 47: A Bright Future

As they made their way back home, Clara and Javier were filled with hope. They knew the road would continue to be difficult, but they were ready to face whatever came. With each step they took together, the love they felt for each other grew stronger.

The journey toward forgiveness and rebuilding was not complete, but they were determined to move forward, holding hands, guided by the love they had cultivated through hardship.

With her son in her arms, Clara looked at Javier and smiled.

They had overcome the pain, and although the future was uncertain, they would face it together, because in the end, love always finds a way.

Chapter 48: The Last Passage

The sound of the baby's laughter filled the room, a soft, familiar melody that enveloped the house. Clara sat in the living room, watching her son play on the floor. He was so full of life, so full of pure energy, that she found it hard to believe everything they had been through to get to this moment. The feeling of peace embraced her, a peace she hadn't known in a long time.

Javier entered the room, a cup of tea in his hand, and sat down next to her. They leaned towards the floor, watching their son together, who was trying to stand up with his small, wobbly hands.

Each of those moments reminded them that life continued to move forward, slowly but surely, and that, despite the difficulties, they had arrived there. Together.

"Look at him, he's growing up so fast," Clara whispered, her eyes full of tenderness.

Javier nodded. His hands sought out hers, intertwining them in silence. No words were needed.

The months of therapy, the long and painful conversations, the nights of insomnia... all that effort had been worth it. Because right now, there, in front of them, was their future. Their son, that little life that had changed everything, reminded them that they could move forward, no matter what had happened in the past.

Their relationship had taken unexpected turns, but now it felt stronger. Clara, though still carrying emotional scars, had learned to forgive in a deeper way. It was not an instant act or an easy forgetting, but a daily choice.

Javier, for his part, had not only changed for her or for the baby, but because he had also learned to forgive himself. He had taken responsibility for his mistakes, but he had also decided not to live anchored in them.

That day was special. Clara hadn't mentioned it before, but she felt she had to close a cycle, something she needed to do before the sun set.

He stood up and walked over to the shelf where he kept a small wooden box that he had kept closed for a long time. Javier watched it silently, intrigued.

"What is that?" he asked, with a mixture of curiosity and caution.

Clara opened the box, revealing letters. Letters she had written to herself during the darkest weeks of her life, when she had been sure that she could not overcome her problems. The words on those papers held so much pain that she had never had the courage to read them again. Until now.

"These letters... I wrote them when I thought everything was lost. When I thought I could never forgive you, that we could never be happy," she said, holding them in her hands. "But they have no power over me anymore. I no longer feel that weight, that darkness."

Javier approached and gently took her arm.

—Clara... you don't have to do it if you're not ready.
She looked at him and smiled. It was a smile full of serenity, of acceptance.

—I'm ready, Javier. Because I'm not the same person who wrote these letters anymore. And I want us to burn this past together, as a symbol that we've changed. We don't need to carry this pain around with us anymore.

They went out into the garden, where the sky was beginning to turn warm shades of red and gold with the sunset. Javier prepared a small bonfire, and together, in silence, Clara threw the letters one by one into the fire.

The flames rose, consuming the words that had once been their prison, turning them to ashes.

As the fire crackled and the paper disintegrated, Clara felt an indescribable release. She was no longer afraid. Not of what had happened, nor of what was to come. What had once been a source of anguish was now just part of their story, a story that had made them both stronger.

Javier hugged her from behind, wrapping his arms around her as they watched the flames.

—Thank you for giving me a second chance —Javier whispered.

"Thank you for not giving up on us," Clara replied, resting her head on his chest.

The fire slowly died out, but the bond between them felt stronger than ever. They had come a long way, and although they didn't know what challenges would come, they knew they would face them together.

That night, as they put her son to bed in his crib, Clara looked at Javier with eyes full of hope.

—You know, I think for the first time in a long time, I'm excited for what's to come. Everything we've been through has prepared us for this moment.

Javier kissed her softly on the forehead.

—Yes, and we will do it well. We are not perfect, but that is what makes us real.

Clara smiled, and together, they closed the door to her son's room.

The future awaited them, full of uncertainties, but also of infinite possibilities. And although the road would never be easy, they knew that, in the end, they had found something deeper than forgiveness: they had found the true meaning of being together.

That was their true ending: not an idealized perfection, but a life built on the ruins of what they once thought was lost, transforming pain into strength, fear into trust, and love into the foundation of their new life.